Praying with

David Pountain was ordained a Baptist minister in 1961 and
has served churches in Lancashire, Cheshire and Gloucestershire.

He is currently Editorial Secretary of the Baptist Missionary
Society.

To
the many extraordinary
men and women
who, during 200 years
of Baptist Missionary Society work,
have sacrificed
their time
their energy
their health
and even their lives
in answering Christ's Great Commission
to "make disciples".

Praying
with God's People

Spreading Spiritual Support across the World

by
DAVID POUNTAIN

Marshall Pickering
An Imprint of HarperCollins*Publishers*

Marshall Pickering is an Imprint of
HarperCollins*Religious*
Part of HarperCollins*Publishers*
77–85 Fulham Palace Road, London W6 8JB

First published in Great Britain
in 1992 by Marshall Pickering
1   2   3   4   5   6   7   8   9

Copyright © 1992 David Pountain

David Pountain asserts the moral right to be
identified as the author of this work

A catalogue record for this book is
available from the British Library

ISBN 0 557 02623 5

Typeset by Avocet Typesetters, Bicester, Oxon

Printed and bound in Great Britain by
HarperCollinsManufacturing Glasgow

CONDITIONS OF SALE

This book is sold subject to the condition that it
shall not, by way of trade or otherwise, be lent, re-sold,
hired out or otherwise circulated without the publisher's
prior consent in any form of binding or cover other
than that in which it is published and without a
similar condition including this condition being
imposed on the subsequent purchaser.

Contents

Preface

"Go, then, to all peoples everywhere and make them my disciples . . ."
MATTHEW 28:19 – The Great Commission.

Two hundred years ago William Carey, "the father of modern mission", challenged British churches to take Christ's Great Commission seriously. Not only did he help found the Baptist Missionary Society, becoming its pioneer missionary, his vision inspired others to follow suit. The Church Missionary Society, the London Missionary Society, the British and Foreign Bible Society and many others in Europe and America entered enthusiastically into the new age of mission.

In 1792, missionary work was about the churches of Europe and North America taking the good news of God's love in Jesus Christ to the millions who had never heard. Two hundred years later the Church has grown into a truly worldwide community of God's people. The old missionary societies now see themselves as partners with the new and growing churches of Africa, Asia and Latin America. They are in the business of sharing resources, people and ideas with the national churches, so that they can be effective in mission. In the same way, the churches at home, in this decade of evangelism, are beginning to learn that they can be receivers in mission from the world Church, as well as givers.

It is in this spirit that we offer this book of prayers and meditations, most of which were written especially for the Baptist Missionary Society. It is our hope that they will help churches and Christians to feel part of the world Church, in its work and mission, as they set about "Praying with God's People".

While many of the prayers in this book are written with a particular country in mind, the situations they describe may occur in many other places, and so other place names can be substituted as the individual need arises.

Catching
the Vision

Catching the Vision

William Carey insisted, in the face of arguments to the contrary, that Christians were obliged to "use every lawful method to spread the knowledge of Christ's name". Two hundred years later, many Christians remain unconvinced. There is a very real need to understand that all Christians belong together in the world Church, sharing all aspects of its total ministry. The following prayers and meditations are designed to help us catch that vision.

Love Let Loose in the World

"The Word became a human being and, full of grace and truth, lived among us." JOHN 1:14

Heavenly Father,
as your creative, saving and loving Word
    was made flesh
    in the life of your son
let loose in the world
so that all can see your glory
– full of grace and truth –
so may your Word be alive in us,
incarnate in our speaking, thinking, doing,
witnessing still to a saving, concerned love
for all your children.

New Life

*"Be concerned above everything else with
the Kingdom of God and with what he requires
of you, and he will provide you with all
these other things."* MATTHEW 6:33

Lord,
we long
   for changes at home,
   for new life in our churches,
   for growth and new members
just as we pray for the worldwide
   work of the Church.

Show us again
where we must begin
   not in working for success in our plans
   but in seeking first
your Kingdom and your righteousness.

The Human Face of Mission

*"Peace be with you. As the Father sent me,
so I send you."* JOHN 20:21

So, Lord, you use people
in your mission of love
    not thunder and lightning
    not floods or plagues
just people – ordinary people
    like Andrew and Simon
       and James and John,
    like Debbie and Gerry
       and Pam and Bill –
people you call, "Come, leave
    your nets, your desks, your fields,
    your banks, your jobs, your homes
       to follow me
    in teaching and healing and caring,
    ministering to the needs of many,
    suffering in love for the world."

Thank you, Lord,
    for the human face of mission,
    for calling people we know,
    for calling people like us,
    for calling us,
       to mission.

For the world Church

We thank you, Lord,
for the nature of your Church,
where there is no "us and them",
where all people of all races, languages and clans,
belong together,
because we all belong to you.

We thank you, Lord,
for the sharing of your Church,
where individual skills and talents
are knitted together into one lively body,
active in a loving, caring ministry
to the many needs of the world.

We thank you, Lord,
for the family of your Church,
where each can learn from the other
and grow in faith
through the experience of brothers and sisters
in other places within the world.

★   ★   ★

Lord,
we pray for every nation and race;
may we
by our actions and lifestyle
proclaim that
all people everywhere
are our brothers and sisters,
whatever their country,
their city,
their tribe,

whatever their education,
their custom,
their tradition,
whatever their circumstances,
their religion,
their colour.

★ ★ ★

One world
is what you created,
but men and women
have torn it apart
in the search
for riches, power
    and influence.

One world
is what you long for,
die for,
lovingly in Jesus
who stretches wide his arms
    to gather all to you.

One world
is why you made your Church
to be Christ's body
living, working, dying,
agents of your healing
    and reconciliation.

Go and Tell

Lord,
you said: "Go and tell . . ."

"Go out", you say.
"Tell humankind", you say.

"Enter a torn and terrifying world", you say,
    when all I want is peace somewhere,
    away from all the
        clamorous,
        clanging,
        grinding noise
of modern times.

Lord,
can you repeat that work with
    hiding,
    crouching,
    fearful men
in a quiet room,
afraid to face a crucifying world,
yet lifted by your resurrection life,
to turn the ancient world
right upside down?

Real for Me?

Lord Jesus,
you lived on this earth
   and gave time to all people.
You had a special place
   for the poor
   and the outcast.
You have felt
   the oppressive, screaming hurt
      of forlorn and bewildered people,
         in your own nailed flesh and bones.
What do you want me to do
now that it has become real for me?

What Do You Want?

Lord,
what do you want of us?
We've sat in church
   and listened to your Word.
We've sung our hymns
   and prayed our prayers
   and in obedience
      met around your table.
We've read our papers,
   watched the telly news
      and sometimes shed a tear
      at the cruelties we see.
Yet you want more?
   Lives moved to action and commitment?
   Lives lived in service of others?
   Lives which call you Lord
      and follow where you lead
         in work to bring the world to life?

The Mourners

"Happy are those who mourn . . ." MATTHEW 5:4

There are those who mourn,
   grieve over the world's evil,
   shout loudly against injustice,
   weep over illness, pain and death . . .
And Jesus wept over Jerusalem.

There are those who protest,
   wave banners high,
   write angrily to the press,
   "Someone, somehow should put things right . . ."
And Jesus wept over Jerusalem.

There are some who serve,
   see a need and humbly help,
   hear a cry and share Christ's love,
   walk with him
      who wept over Jerusalem,
      died outside its walls,
   but never ceased to love and serve.

Lord, bless all who mourn,
   but also love
      and seek and serve and care.

The Humble

"Happy are those who are humble . . ." MATTHEW 5:5

Power matters in this world?
    the power of status and authority,
    the power of money and position,
    the power of education and knowledge.
Forget self and be trampled to the ground.

And we like to be liked,
    to be loved for our giving,
    to be thanked for our serving,
    to be praised for our concern.
Forget self and be taken for granted.

There are not many who are humble,
    really and truly humble,
    humble enough to forget the self,
        carry a cross,
        and follow Christ.

Lord, bless all those who are humble,
    who give and seek no gratitude,
    who serve and never wait for thanks,
    who love without a thought of praise,
    who, hurt, never seek revenge
        but follow him
    who was "meek and lowly in heart".

What God Requires

"Happy are those whose greatest desire is to do what God requires . . ." MATTHEW 5:6

That's hard, Lord!
   knowing what you require,
   understanding your will,
   hearing your Word for today.

So many others compete for our attention
   suggesting
      political ways,
      scientific ways,
      social ways,
      violent ways
   for the world to be saved.

And we confess that we are good at dressing up
   our own ideas in theological language,
   believing that
      our thoughts are your thoughts,
      our will is your will,
      our ways are your ways.

Bless all who seek after true righteousness,
   whose greatest desire is to do what you require,
   who feel the hurt of the world as you feel,
   who care with hearts that long for the healing of men and
      women in body, mind and spirit,
   who follow him whose way is service, sacrifice and love.

The Merciful

"Happy are those who are merciful to others . . ." MATTHEW 5:7

It's easier
  to judge,
  to condemn,
  to reject,
  to savour someone's downfall
than to show mercy,
for mercy is a divine quality,
an attribute of God himself
and we are only human after all.

"Love your enemies,
do good to those who hate you,
bless those who curse you,
and pray for those who ill-treat you
. . . be merciful just as your Father is merciful."

Lord, we can't do it without your help,
for you know how
  to turn feelings of kindness into action,
  to transform pity into gracious deeds,
  to show love to the loveless "that they might lovely be".

Lord, draw close to us and bless us,
  so close that our lives may be one with yours,
  so close that our thoughts may be your thoughts
  so close that our actions may be your actions,
  so close that we may always "be merciful just as our
    Father is merciful".

The Pure in Heart

"Happy are the pure in heart . . ."
MATTHEW 5:8; LUKE II:37-41

He smelled,
   hair tangled and uncombed,
   shoes scarred and unbrushed,
   jeans torn and unwashed . . .
and he sat by me – in church!

He prayed aloud,
   forgive me for my thoughts this week,
   my impure, low-down, dirty thoughts,
   my envious, scheming, greedy thoughts,
   wash me clean . . .
and he smelled
and sat by me – in church!

He walked outside,
   and gently led an old man by the arm,
   "I'll see you home and sort you out,
   cook your meal and cut your lawn."
   He passed me as I left the church . . .
   and he smelled!

The Lord said: "Now then, you Pharisees, you clean the
outside of your cup and plate, but inside you are full of
violence and evil . . ."

Lord, save us and all your people from empty ritual
   and sham respectability.
Cleanse our hearts,
   make pure our thoughts,
   open wide our lives in service
     to the needs of others.

The Peacemakers

"Happy are those who work for peace."
MATTHEW 5:9; PHILIPPIANS 4:1–9

Not those,
   who long for peace
   or plead for peace
   or even keep the peace,
but those
   who reconcile,
   create goodwill
   and work for peace in every place
are blessed of God
and called his kin.

So, Lord, may we
   who dare to pray for peace be those
   who break down walls that shut folk out,
   who soothe the wounds that sear their souls,
      working with him they call the Prince of Peace
to bind up shattered lives into a loving whole.

The Persecuted

"Happy are those who are persecuted because they do what God requires . . ." MATTHEW 5:10

Lord, isn't it enough
    to love our neighbours
    to forgive our enemies,
    to walk the extra mile,
    to do what you require,
    to be your disciples?
Why put us off by talk of crosses
      and of persecution?

Forgive us, Lord,
    remind us when we are hurt
      by the words of others
      by silence or rebuke,
      by outright rejection even,
    that we face nothing alone
    and that the one who died on the cross
    shares all that we have to face.

The Power of Love

"Every power and authority in the universe is subject to Christ as head." COLOSSIANS 2:10

Thank you, Lord,
for these words of hope
because sometimes
other forces seem to be in control
   – economic power
     to enrich a thousand
     and beggar millions
   – political power
     to free the few
     and bind the many
   – people power
     manipulated and misdirected
     by the cunning and corrupt.

Lord,
in our world,
where forces out of control
threaten to overwhelm whole continents,
hasten the day when every authority
shall bow down before the power of your love.

The Power of Prayer

"The prayer of the righteous person has great power in its effect." JAMES 5:16

Lord of the Church,
we confess that it is tempting
  to think in terms of numbers,
  to boast about size and
  to be proud of the great host
    of Christians around the world.

Show us again how your Church began
with a small group of frightened men,
  ineffective and powerless
  so it seemed,
but who "turned the world upside down"
  in the power of prayer
  and in the strength of your spirit.

No Not Me

As the Father sent me so I send you.

No, not me,
definitely not me
   for your mission,
   for your work in the world,
that's for them –
   for the good,
   for the gifted and special,
not for me.
I'm not special
– am I?

Yes,
you're special,
unique,
no one else is like you
whom I send.

No, not me,
I'm no teacher,
   no preacher,
   no big rally speaker.
I blush and I stammer,
I have no pulpit manner,
they won't listen to me
– will they?

That's what Moses said . . .

                                                  Praying with God's People

No, not me,
I'm a sinner,
no winner,
a big non-beginner,
I am lost,
I'm unclean,
not fit for your scheme
– am I?

That's what Isaiah said . . .

No, not me,
I'm too young
and know nothing of love.
I'm naïve,
I'm untaught,
without words
and deep thought.
I'm not ready just yet
– am I?

That's what Jeremiah said . . .

But . . .

No more excuses!
I want you
as you are,
at home or abroad,
for my mission of love
to this world of great need.

Take Time

Take time!
What time?

In our church
   there's no time,
it's gone,
   planned away
in meetings
   for finance,
   for building and heating,
in rotas
   for flowers,
   for coffee and cleaning.

There's the prayer group,
   the house group,
   the singing and praise group;
   the meetings for planning
     for harvest and Christmas.

We've secretaries,
   treasurers,
   agendas and lists
for children and grans,
for women and men,
for toddlers and play groups,
for classes and crêches.

We're busy,
we're active,
a church that's attractive;
but what have we left
when we've sorted things out
    and managed our time
to think,
    of the world,
    of its greed and its pain,
    of people in need
        of the Gospel of love?

Give, Give, Give

Give, give!
They want me to give,
  to the blind and the deaf,
  to the hungry and sick,
  to the elderly poor
    and the disabled child.

Give, give!
She's there by the shops
  with her guilt-making pleas
  as she rattles her tin
  and offers me stickers
    to show to the world
    how generous I've been.

"Give, give!"
says the pastor each week,
  "to the manse roof account,
  to the church heating bill,
  to the new organ fund
    and the damp-rot appeal."

"Give, give!"
says the misionary man,
  "to the church overseas
    which is struggling and poor,
  to outreach,
  to mission,
    that others may hear
      of God's care
      and God's love for them all."

Give, give!
They want me to give
    'cos they say I am rich
        in a world of the poor
    and I'm tired of it all
    I have "giving fatigue", but . . .

"Give, give!"
says the man on the cross,
    not in words but in deeds
        as he bleeds,
        as he dies,
    in love for the world,
    who though rich became poor,
    who never gives up
        as he gives us his all.

God's Surprises

"You shall give him the name Jesus, for he will save his people from their sins." MATTHEW 1:21

Father,
you are a God of surprises,
you meet us when we least expect it
and in places we could never foresee;
but this is the most surprising place of all –
    a stable, a manger, a baby,
    a crying, helpless, vulnerable child.

Thank you, Father,
    for taking the risk,
    for coming down to earth,
    for bringing us down to earth,
        as we see your face
        in the features of a child.

Life for the World

Wine of the grape
running red
pressed hard from the fruit.

Blood of the Lord
running red
squeezed cruelly from his hands and side.

Life flowing free
God's life for the world.

Love reaching out
God's love for us all.

The cost of salvation;
the price of forgiveness;
the gift of new life;
the call to freedom
   from all that enslaves.

Praise be to you,
O Lord Jesus Christ;
thank you for setting us free.

To the Friends at Home

a letter from an overseas Christian
who is living in Britain

For three months I've been in this place
so I thought it was time that I wrote
of my thoughts and my hopes,
of my fears and my tears,
of my efforts to live and to cope.

The church where I'm based is real strange,
it's not what I'm used to at all.
Oh, they sing lively songs
and there's lots going on
but there's something quite radically wrong.

All around there are folk without faith,
young people with nothing to do,
the lonely, the homeless,
the unemployed hopeless,
the prosperous who couldn't care less.

But the church doesn't seem to belong
to the people who live all around;
the members are pious,
all smug and self-righteous,
without any urge to reach out.

They've plenty of money as well,
the Sunday collections are grand,
but they spend it on buildings,
on comfort and trimmings,
not on telling the world about God.

Praying with God's People

No wonder the churches are small,
they haven't a relevant word;
their lifestyle is wrong,
and their vision has gone
of God's mission of love to the world.

Their view of the world is confined,
they see little outside of their walls;
their concern is for self
and for comfort and things;
they are deaf to the cry of the poor.

So that's where I am, my dear friends,
in an alien culture and land;
far away from the warmth
of my village and friends,
may the Lord keep me safe in his hands.

I value your thoughts and your prayers
that my faith may be kept true and strong;
that Christ's mission of love
to the whole of the world
may be shared by us all once again.

Praying
with Missionaries

Praying with Missionaries

How do we pray for missionaries? "God bless their work" is obviously not enough because it is our work too. They are sent from our churches and are part of our missionary outreaching. If we take time to know them, to read their letters, to understand the situations of their work, we can begin to pray with some intelligence not only for them but with them. The prayers which follow are of both kinds. Sometimes we pray for them and sometimes we enter into the prayers, the cries which they utter.

Home and Overseas

*"Christ's message in all its richness must live
in your hearts. Teach and instruct each other
with all wisdom."* COLOSSIANS 3:16

Home and overseas, not separate
but part of the whole,
which is sharing the "good news"
of God's love in Jesus Christ
with people everywhere.

Lord,
we thank you that as churches
we disciple and nurture and send
Christian workers overseas.
Help us to be as faithful
    in our prayer and concern
    and support of their work
when they are far from our sight;
and when they come home
feeling tired and drained
    and spiritually weary
help us to listen with sympathy,
    to learn from them eagerly,
    and to care for them lovingly.

The Missionary Call

"He has been raised from the dead and is going on ahead of you . . ." MATTHEW 28:7

The risen Lord,
not in the grave,
never where we want him,
not ours to hold down
    and worship in a dead place,
but always going on ahead
to fresh places of loving service,
meeting new people in their need
and calling us by name
      to follow.

"That the world may believe . . ." JOHN 17:21

And are you, Lord Jesus, still praying
    that we may be one in your love,
like you with the Father uniting
    that all in the world may believe?

And are you still patiently working
    with people who squabble and split,
their backs on the world ever turning
    on people you died to forgive?

Lord Jesus,
keep on praying for us,
keep on working for us,
transform today's sad group of disciples,
as you changed your mixed up band of apostles,
and create a Church
> united in love
> linked in service,
> one in mission
to a world that longs to believe.

In Training

Lord God,
your servants are training
for overseas service
  on professional courses,
  in missionary colleges,
  at language school,
  and in quiet preparation
    as they commune with you.

They are conscious
of their weakness
in the face of the work
which lies ahead.

Help them to trust in your strength,
and to go forward
where you lead,
humbly and gladly.

May they be worthy of your calling.

Getting Ready to "Go"

So much to do Lord –
    passports,
    visas,
    papers for this,
    papers for that,
  and the bags to pack
    not for two weeks
    but for a year or so –
I've forgotten something, I know
–
    the ticket
    and the times of the flight!

Lord,
    what a rush,
    what a panic,
    there's no time to think
    of the flight and arrival
      and the work
      you have called me to do!

Learning a Language

Lord,
it's hard,
this new language
you've given me to learn,
but thank you
for helping me
   to speak to people,
   to buy in the market,
   to say a simple prayer,
   to read your word.

But it's not just the language,
it's the meaning
   behind the words,
the feelings,
     thoughts,
     associations,
the history of these people.

I'm learning,
     using,
     speaking
their words,
but they're not yet mine,
they don't express
   what I'm thinking
and folk don't hear
   what I'm saying.

Forgive me, Lord –
   in my speaking
   make me as patient
     as those who listen,
and in your good time
bring me to the place
"where the words
have meaning".★

★ Quote from *The Cocktail Party* by T. S. Eliot

Missing Home

It's hotter today
and the market
is swarming
  with people
  and beggars
  and flies.

Food is scarce
  and I'm "different",
  and they haggle
  and giggle
  and want me to pay
  much more than it's worth.

O Lord,
I miss Sainsbury's
  and Tesco's
  and fridges
  and freezers
  and taps
  and cool showers
  and . . .

But this is where I am,
the place where you want me to be
and here I shall stay
until you tell me
to go elsewhere.

And if I miss my church back home –
   the worship
   the singing,
   the meeting,
   the sharing –
thank you for their prayers
   which sustain
   and refresh
   and help me to be your person
     in this place.

Missing the Children

Lord,
we can't wait
for the children
to come back.

It's hard
   not seeing them,
   not watching them grow,
   not being there when they need us,
   not living together as a family.

Thank you
   for the hostel
      where they live,
   for the school
      where they mix
         with children from many lands
and bless those
   who care for them,
   who are as mother and father,
   who love and care and tend them.

Thank you
   for the schools back home,
and bless
   their teachers
   their guardians,
   the local churches,
      who watch over our older children.

Thank you
   that we shall see them soon –
   will we be like strangers
      to each other?

Lord, keep them safe as they travel
   and reunite us as a family
   soon . . .

For Physical Health

Lord,
will she understand
if I refuse
the drink prepared
    especially for me,
the meal made ready
in the hope
    that I would come?

I know that she is poor
and food like this has cost
    much more than she can spare.
But is the water pure?
And those insects
    on the food,
where have they been?

I will accept this meal
prepared by loving hands
and blessed by simple,
    thoughtful prayers.
And will you protect me, Lord,
    this time,
        from worms and bugs,
        from pains and cramps
        from jaundice, fever
            and a host of other ills,
to free me for your work
    today and every other day?

A Doctor on his Rounds

What a journey, Lord!
Five hours already
  since we left
and, when we've
  changed this wheel,
  repaired the bridge,
  diverted round the flooded road,
two hours from now,
they'll be there,
  waiting,
  expectant,
  anxious,
  ready for me to
    operate,
    dispense,
    inject,
    treat their ills,
    heal in the name of Christ.

Lord,
I'm tired already
and, as I pray for safety
  on this journey,
I pray also for
  strength,
  alertness,
  freshness
to aid those skills
you have called me to use
among these people.

For Workers in a Development Project

"A small farm" Lord
– Not large enough
to feed a state,
a continent,
a hungry world.

Lord, take this project
as you took the loaves and fish,
bless its work
and feed a multitude.

Getting on with Local Christians

Lord,
you told me
to take up my cross
   and follow you,
but I didn't think
it would be quite
   so difficult
to be your servant
   in this place.

Forgive me my arrogance;
So often
I think
I know better
than those
who have lived here
   all their lives
and who know
how the people think
   and feel
   and understand
     their world.

Forgive me my superiority;
believing
that I have all the answers,
that I have come
   only to give
and that there is nothing
   to learn
   from these people
   I have come to serve.

Lord,
you humbled yourself,
you took the form of a servant –
help me to be a servant also
and humble enough to listen
    to what the national Christians
        are saying,
    to learn from their example,
    to grow in faith
        through the experience
        of working with them.

Why Am I Here?

This country is crying out for help!
People are sick and there are few doctors.
Children are hungry,
but the land which should feed them
    is eroding away.
They would willingly learn,
if there were those who
    could teach.
So that's why I'm here,
    to work with all my heart,
to heal and feed and teach.

O but it's hard, Lord,
    battling against misunderstanding,
    fighting the harshness of mountain, wind and storm,
    making sense out of confusion,
    continuing to serve in the face of ingratitude.
It's hard, working with my fellow human beings!

Teach me to work as for you and not for people,
may I know that even when I give my all,
it is nothing beside your gifts for me;
may I share that love which cares and serves
and never fails when people reject and spurn;
may I serve and in serving bring glory to
my Lord and not myself.

On Home Assignment

Father,
We look at the vast range of work
done by those we call missionaries –
people serving in so many ways
and in so many places
    caring work and teaching work,
    pioneering work and administrative work,
    work within congregations
    and work wherever people are
        in projects, hospitals, prisons,
        in schools and colleges
and all this in different countries
working in your Name
and by your Spirit.

Father,
some of these workers are home now,
    worshipping with us,
    seeking refreshment and renewal,
    sharing their experiences,
    giving us a vision of world mission,
    reminding us of our privilege and responsibility
        of sharing in your mission of love.

Father,
be with us all,
    equipping us for your work
    and helping us to see beyond the work itself
        to its purpose –
    that men and women and children
    should know you
    and respond to you through Christ,
    and that human need should be met.

★ ★ ★

Lord,
we thank you
for those
who have said "yes"
to your call
and have been serving you
overseas.

We pray for those
who are now home
for a time,
many feeling
    spiritually drained,
    mentally weary,
    and physically tired.
May their time at home
be one of renewal
and re-creation,
as they both minister
and are ministered to
within the churches of
Britain.

For Missionaries at Home

"Run the great race of faith and take hold of eternal life, for to this you were called when you confessed your faith nobly before many witnesses." I TIMOTHY 6:12

Loving Father,
you know
that missionaries are not superhuman,
that they feel all the temptations,
   tensions and inner conflicts
   common to the rest of humanity,
and that because they live and work
   in a different climate and culture
the pressures on them are even stronger.

Father, may they feel you very close to them
as they use this time at home –
   for worship and Christian fellowship,
   for study and reflection,
   for prayer and the development
     of their spiritual life
so that they may "run the great race of faith".

Good News for All

*"How wonderful it is to see a messenger
coming across the mountains, bringing
good news."* ISAIAH 52:7

We praise you, Lord
for those who bring
  good news to the young
    who thirst for knowledge,
  good news to the hungry
    who long to be fed,
  good news to the sick
    who dream of good health,
  good news for all
    that in Christ
    there is healing
    and wholeness
      and newness of life.

For Wisdom in Mission

"If any of you lacks wisdom, he should ask God and it will be given him, for God is a generous giver who neither grudges nor reproaches anyone." JAMES 1:5

Heavenly Father,
   who are we
      to think ourselves wise?
  We confess
     that our vision is limited,
     that our judgements are flawed,
     that our actions are often misconceived.
  We claim to be seeking your will
      in all things
     and yet you know how much our own desires
      get in the way.

Loving Father and ever wise God,
  as we work together
     with Christians around the world
     generously give of yourself
  that in the work of a hospital
     your gentle healing touch may be felt,
  that in the care of devoted pastors
     your understanding love may be experienced,
  that through the skill of teachers
     your wisdom may be realized
  that nothing of ourselves will come between
     you and those we seek to serve.

Results?

*"Will none ever believe without seeing signs
and portents."* JOHN 4:48

But, Lord,
how can we know
that we are doing the right thing
   unless we measure the results of our work?
How can people understand
that you care
   unless they see your love in action?

Forgive us, Lord,
it is true,
sometimes we do seek
dramatic signs of your presence,
but all we truly want to see
are people changed and healed
because they have met you
in the lives and work
   of Christian men and women.

Deliverance

*"I have seen with my own eyes the
deliverance you have made."* LUKE 2:30

And so, Lord,
an old man was overjoyed,
as he saw with his own eyes
the work you had begun in Jesus
to bring about the deliverance
   of men and women
   from all that shackles
      and holds down.

We too rejoice,
for we can see you at work today
   in our world,
   in large city and forest village,
   in developed countries and poor nations,
   in unexpected places;
help us not only to see you
but to join you in your concern
   for people
      and their deliverance.

How Long?

*"Go therefore to all nations and make them
my disciples . . ."* MATTHEW 28:19

Lord, how long should it take?

After two thousand years
as the Body of Christ
alive in the world,
the job's still not done.

As we stop to give thanks
    for missionary work,
    for changed lives,
    for that new and living hope
        in Jesus Christ received
            by countless thousands;
    for churches planted
        in Europe and Asia,
        in Africa and the Americas,
we acknowledge a task unfinished
and recommit ourselves
    to the challenge of Jesus,
    to make disciples of all peoples.

Praying
with People

Praying with People

Our Lord's great commission was to his followers. They were to go to all nations and make disciples. Mission then is mostly about people. Christian men and women serving the needs of others, standing alongside those who suffer, telling the story of what God has done in Jesus Christ, living in love for the sake of others, being the good news for them. The true saints of today are not those who make the headlines, but those who, in spite of their inadequacies, quietly get on with the job that God has given them. Let us pray for some of them.

Praying with Pastors and Leaders

Called to Lead

"Jesus said to him, 'Take care of my sheep'."
JOHN 21:17

Lord,
you have called me to lead others
   in your Church
and I know it's a privilege
   to speak in your name,
but I'm terrified!
What if I get it wrong?
What if I stumble and stammer
   when others wait in need?
What if my words get in the way
   of your Word?

Lord,
you have called me
so give me the words
   I must speak as well,
you have asked me to lead
so prepare me to lead
   in your way.
Keep me
   diligent in Bible study,
   faithful in prayer
and, in all my dealings with people,
     caring and loving.

Too Much!

*"When the day of Pentecost came,
all the believers were gathered together
in one place."* ACTS 2:I

Heavenly Father,
there are times
when the job
   of speaking to people,
   of talking about mission,
   of encouraging men and women
      to become part
      of your mission of love
seems too much
for ordinary human beings
   to tackle,
and then we remember
you have given us
your Spirit of communication
which enables each to hear
   in his own language.

O Spirit of God,
help us to speak
so that others may hear,
and hearing understand,
and understanding obey
   God's Word.

When the Words Don't Come

What can I say
   when the tear begins
   and the widow looks
   and wants to know the reason why?

What can I say
   when the pressure's on
   and the people wait
   for sermons – God-inspired?

What can I say
   when in the chair
   expectant questions
   need their answers from my lips?

What can I say
   when all the time
   a word in life's full,
   varied seasons is required?

What can I say,
   when the words don't come
   and no one's there
   to speak a word to me?

A Parson's Prayer

Sometimes I sit in church on Monday morning,
and sense the solemn quiet of it all:
    silent organ,
    empty pew,
    wrapper of that sweet which took so long
        to cease its plastic rustle,
    table, pulpit, Bible, vase . . .
It's all there –
faith's furniture in storage for another week.

Forgive me, Lord, I see it only my way.
Help me to view it through their eyes –
    the stones made sacred by a lifetime's prayer,
    the walls, which hold within the joy, the hope,
        the sorrow and the love of many folk.
Through those doors they came, as children do,
    wondering, but belonging.
Here they stood to plight their troth,
    and then again in sorrowful remembrance of their dead.
This is their home, where faith and life are bound together.

Eighty now, what's in her mind each week?
Sitting here, the prayer, the word, the book, the hymn
  have helped her face the years of life,
    sometimes tragic,
    mostly hard.
Her joyful faith puts mine to shame.

Forty-five and middle-aged,
children grown and live away,
works hard to earn his bread and run the car –
    "What's life about
    "Where have I been?

"Where do I go?"
Sitting here, he sees me there.
What word of mine can help him, Lord?

The young hide away at the back in this corner,
smiling and nudging and thinking their way.
  "Let's have some changes.
  "Let's brighten things up.
  "Let's pull them to pieces.
  "Let's . . ."
Oh, they frighten me, Lord!
They question my faith and they cause me to think.
  Don't let me cheat them.
  Don't let me fail them.

So here they sit,
the young, the old, the rich, the poor, the educated and
  the ordinary;
    from home and work,
    from school and college,
to worship,
to build up their faith,
to understand their life in you.

Lord, in my impatience, help me to understand how they
feel and to know how they think. May my words spoken
here contain your Word for them, and most of all, help me
to think not of them and me, but of us together, belonging
to your one family and about your great business in the
world.

Pastoral Training

O God of all truth,
we pray for those
training to be pastors.

These are the people
who will serve
   in the name of Christ,
who will read and interpret
   the stories of the Bible.

May they be good students
   asking questions,
   working hard,
not concerned
with their own advancement,
always growing and learning.

So may their student years
prepare them to be leaders
   in your Church.
Equip them
   to speak your Word to people today,
   to foster that encounter with the truth
      which will set men and women free
      to minister as the Body of Christ.

★   ★   ★

Lord Jesus,
   you are the truth.
We pray for those today
   who are studying the Bible,
   equipping themselves

to be teachers,
preachers,
proclaimers of your truth.

And Lord,
when they leave the college classroom
for city church or rural congregation,
may they go on learning
as you teach them
through life's lessons
your Good News for all the world today.

*   *   *

Lord,
we praise you!
for you have given us a Gospel
which can change the lives
of individuals
and of nations.

Lord,
we thank you for those
teaching and studying
in colleges,
institutes
and seminaries
so that the message of your love
may go out
to turn the hearts of men and women to you.

Lord,
we praise you
for your saving, healing Word.

PRAYING WITH CHILDREN AND TEACHERS

Every Child is Precious

Lord,
every child is precious
for every child
is your child.

Give grace
to all who teach
as they deal
with the young
that in everything they do
they may encourage them
to grow in wisdom
as in stature
into the fullness
of Christ himself.

Living and Growing

Lord,
what have we done?
Education is about
  living and growing,
  seeing and undertanding,
  finding your world exciting
    and stimulating,
  stirring the imagination,
  creating a hunger to learn more,
not about examinations and pieces of paper
  to open doors of privilege
    and gain.
Forgive us, Lord,
when we dull young
  and impressionable minds,
when schools become more like obstacles
  blocking the pathway to life
rather than windows
  open to the light
  and colour
  of a fascinating world.
Lord of all knowledge,
be with all those
who are engaged in education,
both those who teach
and those who are taught,
  excite them,
  interest them,
  encourage them,
  enlighten them,
and let them never be satisfied
    with what they know
but always long for more.

The Church of Tomorrow

Lord,
they are the Church of tomorrow
but they are also the Church of today,
if we could only recognize that fact
and harness
    the talents,
    the enthusiasm,
    the vision
of the young
for your work in the world.

Lord,
give us grace
    to listen to what they say,
    to recognize what they can offer,
    to accept gratefully their new ideas,
    to be shifted out of our set ways
in order to mobilize the young
in discipleship and evangelism.

Temptations

*"Be on your guard! I have told you
everything before the time comes."*
MARK 13:23

Lord,
as young people set out in life,
   confronting the many
     problems and temptations
     of developing countries,
   struggling alongside
     many others to survive,
  may they be conscious
   that you are struggling with them,
   that you are sharing their pain
     and understanding their emotions,
   that you are with them and for them.

Youth and Age

"The Holy Spirit whom the Father will send in my name, will teach you everything and remind you of all that I have told you." JOHN 14:26

Loving Lord,
we confess
that sometimes
young people irritate us
    by their lively enthusiasm
        for projects we know are "impossible",
    by the freshness of their vision
        focusing on issues we thought were forgotten,
    by glowing with a faith
        which once was ours.

Understanding Lord,
remove those barriers
    between youth and age
    as together we are taught
        and reminded,
        by the Holy Spirit,
           of all you have said and done.

Praying with Those who Heal

Healing Ministry

Lord,
we pray for all
who are struggling
to combat the many problems
which condemn so many people
to lifelong ill-health.
Guide them in all aspects
of community health and preventive medicine,
bless doctors and nurses working in hospitals
and all those who man clinics
and dispensaries in isolated areas.

For a Christian Hospital

"God is rich in mercy, and because of his great love for us he brought us to life with Christ . . ." EPHESIANS 2:4, 5

Lord,
here is a place
dedicated to life,
where people come
  for healing,
  for an end to pain,
  for a means to overcome disability,
  for a way to live again.
May they also be brought to life
in Christ
as they meet him
in the dedicated lives
of Christian doctor and nurse.

Health Workers

Lord,
those engaged
in medical and health work
have a difficult task.
There are so many people
and so few resources
available to your Church
except your presence, compassion
and care.

Lord,
through your people
working as doctors, nurses
and health workers,
bring to all who need it
your healing, health and wholeness.

Praying for the Oppressed

Praying for Persecuted Believers

*"Here I stand knocking at the door; if anyone
hears my voice and opens the door, I will
come in and he and I will eat together."*
REVELATION 3:20

Lord,
you are ready to sit and eat with anyone!
   anyone who recognizes your voice,
   anyone who invites you in,
      woman, man, child or adult,
      Asian, American, African or European,
      illiterate, well–read, foolish or wise,
      sad, happy, poor or rich,
      sinner or . . . well, we're all sinners
      . . . but you are willing
         to accept us and take tea with us!

We thank you that more and more people
   are recognizing your voice;
and if they hesitate,
   because their families would reject them
      or their village condemn,
if they hesitate to invite you in just yet
   stay with them,
   work with them,
   keep knocking,
until they have courage and confidence
to invite you to sit and eat with them.

Corruption and Oppression

"He will rule his people with justice and integrity." ISAIAH 11:5

Justice and truth –
   of such words, twisted and bent,
     are revolutions made
     and tyrant forces take tight hold;
   by such words, narrowed and cramped,
     are hostages held
     and freedom dies another death;
   from such words, turned inside out,
     excuses flow
     and racist hate destroys another's home.

God of justice and truth,
we praise you
for not speaking in words
that drift away on the wind
but in the person of Jesus,
the Word made flesh,
the way, the truth and the life.

For the Suffering Church

"God is to be trusted."
2 CORINTHIANS 1:18

Heavenly Father,
you are always to be trusted!

Even in the dark, depressing days
of treacherous crucifixion,
when death spits, "No!"
into the face of life
and mocks the light of hope
in dimming eyes
your last
and lasting word
is "Yes!"
to life
in Christ
for all the world.

For Refugees and Others Away from Home

"There was a wedding at Cana-in-Galilee. The mother of Jesus was there, and Jesus and his disciples were also among the guests . . ." JOHN 2:1, 2

Heavenly Father,
thank you for those stories of Jesus
which tell us how he enjoyed life,
how he loved the company of people,
how he had time for them,
at weddings and meals,
   chatting to them,
   listening to them,
   valuing them,
      as you value all people.

Father,
teach us never to forget
that mission is about human beings.
So help us to take time
to pray for people far from their homes,
   refugees in a foreign land,
   students at college or university
      trying to understand a new tongue
      and culture,
   some of them in Britain,
   feeling isolated, vulnerable, lonely;
help us
   to welcome them,
   to talk with them,
   to listen to them,
   to value them,
      and to learn from them.

Praying with Churches around the World

Praying with Churches around the World

The phenomenon of today's world Church is that, after 200 years of reaching out in mission activity, white western Christians within the Euro–American churches are in a minority. And the churches of Africa and in many parts of Asia continue to grow, some of them at a tremendous rate. Our fellow Christians encompass many nations, languages and races. So the following prayers can only be examples. Although some mention particular countries, they may well fit other situations. Feel free to adapt them.

THE WORLD CHURCH

Christ's Body

*"We who are united with
Christ, though many, form one
body, and belong to one
another as its limbs and
organs."* ROMANS 12:5

One body and one mission
    to the whole of humanity,
all working together
    as Christ's body,
alive and active
    in the world,
with one purpose –
to reach out to others
in loving Christian service
    and witness . . .

Lord,
by your Spirit,
turn this dream
into a reality.

Not by Bread Alone

"I am the bread of life." JOHN 6:48

Lord,
in a country like . . .
where the need for daily bread
    is more than obvious
we pray for the total ministry
    of the Church.
Bless those engaged in a ministry
of care, comfort and relief,
but strengthen too the witness of those
who open the scriptures
and show that human beings
"cannot live on bread alone".

Ready and Alert

"Your minds must be stripped for action and fully alert." I PETER 1:13

So, Father,
we must be ready and alert
just like your prophets of old,
seeing your hand in the events of the day,
condemning evil and injustice,
speaking your Word,
pointing out your way
    through unselfish lives,
        dedicated witness,
            and loving, Christlike service.

And this we pray,
for Christians in . . .
that they may be fully alert
    to the dangers and temptations
        confronting them,
and that they may be ready for action
and uncompromising in witness
    to their Lord Jesus Christ.

A World Vision

"King of kings and Lord of Lords."
REVELATION 19:16

That's the aim, Lord,
that's our vision
    in a world that's divided,
    in a world that's confused,
    in a world without peace,
    in a world in pain,
    in a world that's lost its way,
we long for the day,
we work together for the day
when people
of every tribe and nation
shall acknowledge you
as King of kings and Lord of lords.

Praying with God's People

For the Church in . . .

*"There must be no limit to your goodness,
as your heavenly Father's goodness knows no
bounds."* MATTHEW 5:48

Loving Lord,
we confess
that we often set limits
to our "goodness";
   we put conditions on Christian giving,
   we stop loving the unlovely,
   we look for rewards for our service.

Lord,
whose reward was cruel nails and a cross,
may the caring work
of Christian people in . . .
as in every other place,
be as the goodness of their Heavenly Father
      and know no bounds.

For Small and Isolated Christian Communities

"Hold the Lord in awe, and serve him in loyalty and truth." JOSHUA 24:14

Loving Lord,
uphold Christians
who are surrounded by many who
    follow other beliefs,
    hold other gods in awe,
    and claim theirs as the only way.

Give them wise words,
as they meet and talk with
    Muslim, Hindu, Sikh or Buddhist,
that they may be able to give a reason
    for the hope that is within them.

Strengthen them when they are tempted
    to lower their standards,
    to compromise their faith
        or to deny their Lord;
may they always serve you
    in loyalty and truth.

AFRICA

Lord Jesus,
before ever we know
  or even begin to understand,
you are there
  at the heart of human suffering and need;
in Africa's growing cities
  and squalid shanty towns,
  sharing the lives of all
    who are trying to cope with poverty
      and hopelessness;
in a country's struggle to pay its way,
  where a nation's bankruptcy is spelled out
  in the privations of ordinary people.

Yes Lord, you are there way before us,
  and we know that you care.
We thank you for those
  who have heard the call to serve
    in your name
    in these places,
  for those who are
    teaching,
    counselling,
    advising
      and pastoring,
    building up your people in faith;
  for those
    who by their service are helping
      in the development of Africa,
    bringing new ideas
      to the growing of crops
      and the pursuit of rural crafts.

Alive and Growing

Lord,
Thank you for Africa.
Thank you for
  its colour and life,
  the wealth of the land,
  the joy and the variety of its people,
    and the caring bonds of family and tribe.

Thank you for the Church in Africa,
  alive and growing,
  seeking to be truly African
  and working to meet the needs of people
    in body, mind and spirit.

Give the Church courage
  and strength
  to face the special challenges of today,
and enable its leaders,
  pastors
  and members
    to be part of
    a loving,
      reconciling,
      caring ministry
    to people
      living in the midst
      of economic, social and spiritual need.

Unseen Forces

"For we are not fighting against human beings but against the wicked spiritual forces in the heavenly world, the rulers, authorities, and cosmic powers of this dark age." EPHESIANS 6:12

Heavenly Father,
we pray for the people of Africa,
joyful, caring and full of life
and yet so often
    victims
        of uncaring governments,
        of unseen forces which exploit
            and use
            and keep them poor,
    victims
        of climate and disease,
        of poverty and hunger.

Father,
bless the Church in Africa
as it works alongside the people,
helping them to understand
that your love is strong
and able to defeat
all those powers,
seen and unseen,
which are ranged against them.

Victims of Poverty and Debt

"The Lord, the eternal God, creator of earth's farthest bounds, does not weary or grow faint; his understanding cannot be fathomed." ISAIAH 40:28

Loving Father God,
so many people in Africa are tired,
    exhausted by suffering that has no end,
    faint with hunger that cannot be satisfied,
    worn out and battered by the struggle to live;
through the sacrificial living
of Christian men and women
help them to know
    that you are with them,
    that you understand,
    that you are working for them,
and that the strength, love and care
of the one who never wearies or grows faint
    is always with them.

Young People

"And now he can help those who are tempted, because he himself was tempted and suffered." HEBREWS 2:18

Lord,
it was not angels
you came to help
but people
involved in the struggles of life,
   lifted by hope,
   downed by disappointment,
   tempted at every turn;
so you know how the young people
   of Africa feel
as they strive to better their lives,
as they and their families face
   the problem of raising school fees,
as they are tempted
   to "cheat the system" to gain
     the piece of paper
     which will give them
     future position, income,
       and security.
So may they be conscious
   of your help
   as they try to uphold
     Christian standards.

*   *   *

*"If you have love for one another,
then everyone will know that you are
my disciples."* JOHN 13:35

Lord,
we rejoice
that there are many
in Africa
who have heard your call,
"Follow me",
and have joined you
in your ministry.

As they care for people
who are sick in body
help them to minister also
to their spiritual needs
and to reveal your sacrificial love
in all they do.

ANGOLA

No Easy Task

*"Love is not happy with evil, but is happy
with the truth."* I CORINTHIANS 13:6

Lord,
you have not given to your people
an easy task in any place,
but in Angola it has been doubly difficult.
    Why should they suffer so much
       and for so long?
    Why has it taken so long
       to end their civil war?
Lord, we echo the questions they ask
    and join them in their prayers
       for a lasting peace.

Thank you for their faithfulness too.
They have not found
    in their troubled land
    excuses to do nothing
    but opportunities to serve.
Bless their work
    of teaching and training,
    of healing and caring,
    of witnessing to your love
       in all its fullness.

To Open Eyes

*"You are to open their eyes and turn them from
the darkness to the light . . ."* ACTS 26:18

And so, Lord,
you commission your servants
   to open the eyes of people,
   to turn them from darkness to light,
and that's the task
   which the Christians of Angola
     have accepted willingly
   in spite of war and exile and poverty.

We thank you
   for their compassionate care
     of those hurt by war,
   for their courage
     in speaking your truth
     when others have proclaimed
       a different creed.

Be their guide and inspiration
   as they try to make sense of the problems
     which face their country,
   as they seek to understand
     what their task of mission
       should be.

Living as Your People

They shame us, Lord,
　these Christians in Angola.
We give up so easily
　at the slightest opposition,
　at the first disappointment,
　at the smallest frustration.

Humble us, Lord,
　help us to learn
　　how to work,
　　how to witness,
　　how to live as your people
　from the example of those
　who have returned from exile,
　　rebuilt the Church
　　and have gone on
　　　to reach the unreached,
　　　working for peace,
　　　for justice
　　　and for reconciliation
　　　amongst those
　who are weary of war.

Courage and Faith

Lord,
    we give you thanks
    for the courage and faith
    of many Christians
    in Angola
    during so many years
        of difficulty and turmoil.

We pray
    for true peace in Angola,
    that peace which knows
        no bitterness,
        no secret desire for revenge,
        no division
    but only reconciliation
    and co-operation.

Be with your Church
in Angola,
that in witness
    and in service
she may be an example
to the nation
    of justice,
    of freedom,
    of compassion
        and of Christian love.

Liveliness and Vision

Lord,
  we pray for your people in Angola,
  working within a nation
  torn by war
  and amongst people
  tired of conflict.

We give thanks for
  their liveliness,
  their vision,
  their determination
    to share your love and peace
    with the whole nation.

We pray
  that they may have
    wisdom to understand your will,
    courage to grasp each opportunity
      for witness,
    patience in the face of frustration
      and difficulties.

ETHIOPIA AND THE SUDAN

"I am able to face anything through him who gives me strength. All the same it was kind of you to share the burden of my troubles." PHILIPPIANS 4:13-14

Loving Lord,
we are confident
    that you are with the people in the Horn of Africa
        in all the troubles they face,
        in the political turmoil of their nations,
        in the poverty and hunger
           which is none of their fault;
we are confident
    that you are
        weeping with them,
        suffering with them,
        caring with a broken, loving heart
           for lives which are shattered and lost,
        offering your strength, yourself
           that they may be able to face anything.

Lord,
you have called us to join you
in this ministry of caring love;
show us how we can stand with them,
sharing part of the burden of their troubles.

ZAIRE

Bibles and Books

"Be sure, then, to keep in your
hearts the message you heard from
the beginning." 1 JOHN 2:24

Lord of all knowledge,
we thank you
   for books,
   for writers,
   for translators
     and printers,
and for all the ways
in which we can read
   and learn
    and deepen our understanding
      of the Christian faith.

And with Christians in Zaire,
who have so few books and Bibles,
we pray for those
who are busily writing, translating
and making available
good Christian literature
so that your people can grow
in wisdom.

Women's Work

Caring God,
we thank you for equipping
the women of Zaire
with gifts of ministry and service,
so that the Church
is strengthened to serve
those who are in prison and hungry,
those who are in hospital and frightened,
those who cannot read but long to learn of you.

So, Lord,
help the women of Zaire to enrich the life of the
people and witness to your compassionate love.

Health Work

Lord,
in the vast land of Zaire
the Church has set about a daunting task
of bringing health and healing to the people.
Progress is slow
and sometimes we doubt
that it is happening at all.
But we praise your name that,
slowly and quietly,
doctors and nurses and health workers
are being trained
and people are learning to trust
what they say and teach and do.

Lord,
through the medical and health work
of Christian personnel
bring wholeness and healing
to those whose lives are marred
   by handicap and disease.

Sharing and Caring

"Share your belongings with your
needy fellow Christians, and
open your homes to strangers."
ROMANS 12:13

Loving Lord,
you remind us
   in so many places
that your mission of love
   is more than slick and easy talk,
that it involves sharing
   the needy lives of people
bringing the hope
of an end to hunger,
ill health
and the burden
   of unrewarding toil.

Bless the work of those in Zaire
who have willingly entered
into this caring ministry.

The River Zaire

Such a long river, Lord,
so many miles
separating Christian centre
from Christian centre
so easy, too easy to live for the self
forgetting the church
in the next district,
at the other end of the country.

Such large parishes, Lord,
so many miles
for the pastors
to travel,
so many people to see,
so many services to take,
too much for one person to tackle.

Lord,
in spite of distance
in the face of busy-ness and overwork
may your people in Zaire be one –
one in hope,
one in vision,
one Church renewed for mission.

ASIA

For this Vast Continent

*"We can approach God with this confidence; if we
make requests which accord with his will, he listens
to us . . ."* I JOHN 5:14

Lord,
in this rapidly changing world
we often stop, bewildered,
wondering where to turn next
    in the task of mission;
sometimes we feel frustrated
when plans come to nothing
and a great opportunity for mission
    just has not worked out.

And so we turn to you
    with our requests for Asia,
    with our pleas for the oppressed Church,
    with our prayers for people in poor countries,
    with our petitions for men and women
        in wealthier nations,
    with our longing for a clear vision
        of true partnership with Christians
        in this vast continent.

Many Faiths

Lord,
it is hard for us to understand
    what it means to be a Christian
    among so many people
    of different faiths;
it is difficult for us to realize
    what it is like
    to live in an area of such vast need;
but we know enough
    to wonder
    what so few Christians can do;
then we remember
    what you said
        about yeast
        and salt
        and mustard-seeds,
        and how you changed
            a small group of frightened men
            in an Upper Room
            into a force
        which turned the world upside down.

Lord,
be with our brothers and sisters in Asia
    so that their strength
        may be stronger than their numbers,
    and their witness
        effective throughout the population.

Half the World

Lord, it's hard
to pray for those we do not know,
to feel for those we've never seen,
to care for those whose voice we've
    never heard.

Half the world's people live in Asia
    and we are neighbours to them,
        these statistical people,
        these anonymous people,
        these curves on the graph
            of the world's this and that –
        and you tell us not to pass by
            on the other side.

Lord, to you
    no one is lost in the crowd,
    you recognize the features of each face,
    you move towards the sound of each one's voice;
so bring alive for us
    the newsprint picture
        of the victim of a flood,
    help us to hear
        the person in the anguished
        sound-track cry of television news,
    give meaning
        to the figures of the annual aid report,
        bring Asia close . . .
        so close
            that we may never even think of passing
            on the other side.

A Minority

Bless, O Lord,
   the Christian Church in Asia,
give to Christians a sure faith
   in places where they are a minority
   amongst the followers
      of Islam,
      of Hinduism,
         or Buddhism.
By their witness
may they make known
   the Lordship of Jesus Christ.

Relieve
all those who suffer
   from flood,
   from famine
      and from the evils
      of repressive governments.

Help the Christian Church in Asia
to be sensitive
   to these needs
and to bring the light
   of your love and care
   into the lives of many.

Energy and Colour

*"My prayer is that our fellowship
with you as believers will bring about
a deeper understanding of every
blessing which we have in our life in
union with Christ."* PHILEMON 1:6

So many countries, Lord,
and so many tongues and
traditions,
     beliefs and superstitions –
such energy and colour
     and countless individuals
     of many races;
we give thanks for the people
     of Asia and the richness they
     contribute to the world.

And your Church, Lord,
     strong and growing in one place,
     small and struggling in another;
thank you for
     the constancy of their faith
     and their sure witness
to your love in so many situations.

BANGLADESH

God's Children

"God's Spirit joins himself to our spirits to declare that we are God's children." ROMANS 8:16

Abba! Father!
  We pray for the Christians of Bangladesh.
  They are all your children,
    and just like Christians in other places
    they worship
    and witness
    and care for the needy.
  But in that poor, overpopulated country,
    surrounded by millions of another faith,
  they must feel
    isolated, vulnerable,
    powerless, at risk from the Muslim majority.
Abba! Father!
  Save them from slavery to fear,
  and by your Spirit
  give them the confidence of knowing
    that they are your children
      through Jesus Christ,
    and that if they have to share
      his suffering
    they will also share his glory.

Walking with Christ

*"Wasn't it like a fire burning in
us when he talked to us on the
road and explained the Scriptures
to us?"* LUKE 24:32

Lord,
you have promised
to be with your disciples
until the end of time,
and it is true
you walk with us
day by day,
often unrecognized,
opening Scripture to us
and deepening our understanding
of your truth.

Lord,
may this be true
for Christians in Bangladesh
as they teach
and are taught,
and try to understand
how they must live
and work and witness
as a small group
surrounded by millions
of another faith.

Spirit of Unity

*"You believed in Christ, and God put his
stamp of ownership on you by giving you the
Holy Spirit he had promised."* EPHESIANS 1:13

Lord,
may the small Christian group
   in Bangladesh
bear the obvious mark
of your Spirit of unity
   and love
as they engage
in a ministry of
healing, care and aid.

Hungry

Lord Jesus,
many people in Bangladesh are hungry,
   with nothing in the larder
   and no bread to spare,
and we long and pray for the day
   when there will be enough
      for everyone to eat,
   when no child will be malnourished,
      and no one die of hunger.

Lord Jesus,
there are many more who are inwardly hungry
   for the things of the Spirit.
You are the Bread of Life,
and without you all hearts go hungry,
   all lives are empty.

Lord Jesus,
help your servants in Bangladesh
   constantly to feed on you by faith
      that knowing the abundant life themselves
      they may be fitted to share the nourishment
         of the Gospel
            with their fellow countrymen.

The Spirit of Service

Lord,
    following your way
    the Church in Bangladesh
    has discovered a spirit of service
    and has embarked on a ministry of care.

Remind your people,
we pray,
that as they are called to serve
they are to go out with the Good News,
the truth you taught,
    and preached,
    and lived,
    and only the Church can do this.

Dignity and Self-reliance

Lord,
  we know
  that much is expected
  of those who possess much.
If we
  as partners
  with the Church in Bangladesh
  are truly doing your will,
  help us to give
  the support they need,
    in prayer,
    in personnel,
    in money.
May the help we offer
build dignity and self-reliance,
rather than aid
  that perpetuates dependence.
All things come from you
and it is of your own
that we can give.

CHINA

Your Church is alive, Lord!
   Alive in China
   as in every other place,
so why are we surprised?
It is your Church!

But we doubt –
many times we doubt,
thinking human power
strong enough
to overwhelm
   the weakness of the cross.

Thank you for
   surprising us,
   shaming us,
   showing up the shallowness
      of our faith.

Thank you
   that the Church in China
   has emerged from obscurity
      strong in faith and purpose.

Lord, give us faith
   to trust that you are with your Church
   in all times of uncertainty,
   equipping your people
   to be living witnesses
      of your love.

INDIA

An Everlasting Kingdom

*"His authority would last for
ever, and his kingdom would never
end."* DANIEL 7:14

Lord,
yours is an everlasting kingdom
that will never pass away,
but sometimes
watching with our earthly eyes
it looks fragile and vulnerable
and ready to break apart,
especially
when Christians don't agree
and struggle for status and authority.

Lord,
hold together the Church of North India
in a unity which is strong in witness
just because of the variety of background
and experience.

A New Creation

"When anyone is joined to Christ, he is a new being, the old is gone, the new has come." 2 CORINTHIANS 5:17

Lord,
to you
no one is insignificant,
but it is easy
to feel forgotten
in India
among the millions
who live there,
if you are young
and want to go to school
or college,
so we thank you for the Church,
part of your new creation,
that is learning to see
people through your eyes
and is caring for the needs
of the young.

Set Free

Lord,
we praise you
that your Spirit sets people free
   from fear and superstition,
   from caste and class,
   from all that holds them down,
to be Christ's lively body
   ministering in a world
      which cries so loud for help.
Lord,
forgive your Church
   for finding other bonds
      to hold folk down,
   for new traditions
      stifling fresh ideas
   for pride of status and fear of
      other faiths.

May the Church in India
be set free
by your Spirit
to share their faith
in a living saviour.

Opposition

*"If the God whom we serve is able to
save us . . . then he will."* DANIEL 3:17

Lord,
some of the Christians in India
know what it means
to be opposed
by people who believe in other gods.

Some have been mocked,
some have had their faith challenged,
some have had their churches burnt to the ground.

Yet they continue to witness to your love,
they still care and love
and offer much to those who need your help.

Thank you, Lord, for their faithfulness, and
be to them always their help and their strength.

Expressing the Gospel

Lord,
we pray for your Church
in India
striving to express your Gospel
in ways that can be understood
by Indian people,
working for sharing
between the urban rich
and the poor of the villages.

KOREA AND SINGAPORE

For Growing Churches in Asia

"Thanks be to God, who continually leads us as captives in Christ's triumphal procession, and uses us to spread abroad the fragrance of the knowledge of himself!" 2 CORINTHIANS 2:14

Thanks be to you, Lord God,
    for leading the Christians of Korea/Singapore
        as captives in Christ's triumphal procession,
    for using them to spread abroad
        the fragrance of the knowledge of yourself.

Continue to use them
    to challenge all that is wrong,
    to uphold everything that is good,
    to bear witness to him
        who alone brings life.

The Marks of the Church

*"To get this done I toil and struggle,
using the mighty strength which
Christ supplies and which is at work
in me."* COLOSSIANS 1:29

Labour and struggle
in the face of persecution
are the marks
of the Church in Nepal,
but all praise be to you,
good Lord,
that they have also known
the victory
of those who struggle
"using the mighty strength
which Christ's love supplies".
We praise you for growth
in numbers
and now for signs of a new freedom
to work and worship as your people.

Impossible

"Jesus looked straight at them and answered, 'This is impossible for man, but for God everything is possible'." LUKE 18:27

Lord, it can't be done
- this task of healing
    which you've given us!
The tracks are narrow and steep
and the mountains get in the way
    of reaching people.
There are too many sick
and not enough doctors and nurses
    and dentists.
But with you, Lord,
all things are possible,
so bless the ministry of healing
in Nepal.

A World Transformed

Lord God,
in a country
where Christians have been told
   not to preach,
   not to speak,
   not to tell others of your love,
may they offer
   by their living
your promise of a world transformed.

May men and women
see in them
your body,
your bride,
loving and compassionate,
humble and holy.

Words "Made Flesh"

We thank you, Lord,
that sometimes
you make it difficult for us to speak,
and force us to live the words
we would have spoken
in loving, caring actions.
May such words "made flesh"
in hydro schemes,
in agriculture, forestry and industry,
speak more eloquently
of your love
than syllables half-heard
and hardly understood.

Keeping Faith

"God keeps faith and will not let you be tested beyond your powers, but when the test comes he will at the same time provide a way out and so enable you to endure." I CORINTHIANS 10:13

Thank you, Lord,
    for keeping faith
        with the Christians of Nepal
        through the years of persecution,
    for standing by them
        in their times of testing,
    for helping them to witness
        through their lives
        if not their words.

Lord,
    keep faith with them now
        as they explore their new-found freedom.
    Stand by them today
        as they are tested by fresh problems.
    Help them to make a good witness
        by matching the quality of their lives
        with the honesty of the words
           they are now free to utter.

SRI LANKA

Looking up

*"But Stephen, full of the Holy Spirit,
looked up to heaven and saw God's glory
and Jesus standing at the right-hand side
of God."* ACTS 7:55

Lord,
there are times
in the middle
of this world's
agonizing and struggle
when we need
to lift up our eyes
from the squalor and tawdriness
of human behaviour
to see your glory,
and to see Jesus,
who knows what life
and struggle and death
on this earth are like.
Give this vision
to the Church in Sri Lanka
that it may be encouraged
in its ministry of reconciliation
within that troubled island.

Building Bridges

"You do not let your anger rage for ever,
for to be merciful is your true delight."
MICAH 7:18

Lord,
be merciful to the island of Sri Lanka,
weary of violence and sudden death,
tired of division and enmity
    between different groups.

Give wisdom to those in positions of power
that they may appreciate
    the anxious fears,
    the dreams and hopes,
      of Sinhalese and Tamil alike,
      and so meet each problem
        with understanding.

And help the small Christian community
in its task of building bridges
of compassion
and reconciliation.

THAILAND

"Man looks at the outward appearance,
but I look at the heart." I SAMUEL 16:7

Such a tiny group of Christians
    in Thailand,
not important at all
    or so it seems,
by all appearance
    insignificant in this Buddhist land;
but we thank you, Lord,
that you look at their hearts,
    not their size,
    not their numbers,
only their love, their sincerity,
    their devotion and commitment.
Anoint them with your Spirit, Lord,
and use them well in the service
of your Kingdom.

EUROPE

An Open Door

*"They stood at a distance and shouted, 'Jesus!
Master! Take pity on us.' "* LUKE 17:12–13

Lord,
you have opened a door into Eastern Europe,
    a door to people who have suffered and suffer,
    a door to a Church which grew strong under threat,
    a door of opportunity to new partnerships,
        to a sharing of resources
        and of mutual help.

Lord,
we hear a cry for help
from east and from west.
Help us to discern your voice
to know what you are saying,
so that in hearing we may obey.

A New Heart

"I will give you a new heart and a new mind.' EZEKIEL 36:26

A mission field
not far away
but close at hand,
our neighbours
in the new and changing Europe,
with problems like our own
paying lip-service
to a glorious Christian past
and searching
for a new and satisfying faith.

Lord, through the life and worship
of your people
give a new heart
and breathe the life of your Spirit
into the crumbling skeleton
of a people's faith.

Lord of the City

O Lord of the city,
  where it is easy
    to feel lonely,
      forgotten,
      isolated,
    among the thousands
    who mill around,
  enable your Church
  to create centres
    of true community,
  where people belong
      and can grow
      and realize
    their full humanity
  as they discover themselves
      and their fellows
  encompassed by your love.

In the Throes of Change

*". . . nation will not lift up sword
against nation nor ever again be trained
for war."* ISAIAH 2:4

Lord, we Christians have such high ideals,
   or are they pious longings
    far beyond the reach of mortal beings?
Over the years of this century,
as Europe's armies battered
   and beat each other down,
    in wars to end all wars,
we have picked up and prayed
   the words of Isaiah.

Lord, help us to take this time
   of change in Europe
to show your hand at work in history
and to reveal your true
and lasting way to peace.

Seeking

*"The first step to wisdom is the fear of the
Lord, and the knowledge of the Most Holy One
is understanding . . ."* PROVERBS 9:10

Europe,
proud of its history,
wealthy in literature and learning,
where reason and science
    fascinate rational minds,
a post–Christian place
where faith belongs
    to yesterday.

Yet, Lord,
some are searching for other ways,
beyond the reach of human minds,
wondering where true wisdom may be found.

Open the hearts, minds, lives
        of all who seek a "knowledge
        of the Most Holy One".

For Eastern Europe

"Speak, Lord; your servant is listening."
1 SAMUEL 3:9

Loving God,
this is a busy world
full of people and noisy movement,
and it is so easy
to be carried forward
by a surging wave of activity
without asking "Why?",
without wondering where we are going
or trying to discover the purpose of it all.
Yet there is so much to be done
in such a short time
in Eastern Europe,
recovering from long years of oppression,
getting used to freedom
and trying to reconstruct their nations.

Gracious

Patient God,
help all your people to stop and listen
that they may hear your word
and discover your will
   for their lives,
   for the Church,
   for their land
     and for the world.

BRAZIL

Not Alone

*"The world will make you suffer.
But be brave! I have defeated the
world."* JOHN 16:33

Lord,
   your work is difficult,
   but then you never said
   it would be easy,
   promising trouble, suffering
      and rejection
   to all who follow you.

But you also promised a "helper"
   and that your disciples would
   not be alone in their
   task of witnessing to your love.

So may your servants
   in Brazil
   be conscious
   of your nearness and help
   and the guidance of your Spirit
   in all they do for you.

Sensitive to Need

*"I was hungry and you fed me, thirsty and
you gave me a drink . . ."* MATTHEW 25:35

Lord,
you came to meet our human needs –
   the poor, the sick, the disabled,
   the broken family,
   those without work,
   the hungry.

May your people in Brazil
be sensitive to the needs of their country,
   needs often unseen and unspoken.
Help them to bring faith, hope and love
   into the lives of many.

Born to Be Free

*"To show that you are his
sons, God sent the Spirit of his
Son in our hearts . . ."*
GALATIANS 4:6

Father God,
so much need,
so many people
    slaves to poverty
in a land of great wealth,
and yet they are your children
born to be free –
    free from hunger,
    free from disease,
    free from ignorance,
    free for life with all its
        exciting possibilities.
Father God,
whose Son died
that people might have life
    in abundance,
through your Spirit
working through the lives
of Christian servants,
liberate the people of Brazil
    for Life.

Economics and Ecology

*"I know, Lord, that you are all-powerful; that
you can do everything you want."* JOB 42:2

Lord God,
you can do all things
so the Bible says!
And can you do something for Brazil
   to help it solve its economic problems,
   to stop the destruction of the forests,
   to prevent an ecological disaster?
Or are you leaving that to people of vision
who have learnt a better way in Jesus Christ,
who have turned away from selfish, wasteful living?

Lord God,
guide the churches of Brazil,
help them to share their knowledge of you –
   great Creator of all that is,
   loving Saviour of the world,
   faithful Sustainer of all you have made –
with the people of their land.

Worthy

"Our Lord and God
you are worthy
to receive glory, honour and power,
for you created all things
and by your will they were given
existence and life." REVELATION 4:11

Dear Lord,
thank you for your people in Brazil
who worship you in their lives
and give you honour and glory by
    preaching your Word,
    healing the sick,
    teaching those who have never
        been able to learn,
    feeding the hungry and
    befriending the lonely and forgotten.

No Other God

"I am the Lord; there is no other god."
ISAIAH 45:5

Forgive your people, Lord.
There is no other god
and yet we worship many idols.
We replace the living, life-giving Lord
with the dead and negative gods
   of money and ambition and success
and so destroy others, your creation
and ourselves.

Lord,
you have given to the Church in Brazil
the joy of sharing the good news of your love,
   in word and action,
with city dweller and landless worker,
with privileged family and needy child.
Help your Church
to make a strong and sure witness
to the only one worthy of worship and praise.

São Paulo

A large, expanding city,
traffic, fumes and noise,
people everywhere
   in towering block,
     suburban home,
     favela slum,
children on the street,
   abused, unloved and lost,
and, Lord, you are there
   long before we notice,
calling us to follow,
to be where you are already
   living with the neglected,
   eating with the poor,
   suffering with the addicts,
crucified again by those
who will not understand.

So Young!

Lord,
    Brazil amazes us.
    It's so large –
      half a continent in size.
    It's so young –
      half the population under nineteen years of age.
    It's so full of energy
      and vitality
      and movement
        as it grows and expands.
    But it saddens us too
      as we see
        its needs,
        its contrasts between rich and poor,
          and the effects
          of a broken economy.

Lord,
    we thank you for the concern
      of Brazilian Christians
    to help all those seeking a new life
      to find it in Christ.
    We praise you for their growing concern
      for the socially deprived,
      and for their missionary zeal
        at home and abroad.
    Help us to be true partners with them.

Such a Mixture!

Such excitement,
   energy,
   belief,
   in a country
     and its future!
Such a mixture of people,
   mostly young,
   mostly poor,
     from all over the world,
    but proud and optimistic.
We pray for them, Lord –
   exploited rubber-tapper,
   ruthless landowner,
   shanty town child,
   city dweller,
     each trying to survive
     amid soaring inflation,
    and open to the Gospel.
Be with the churches,
   with your people,
     as they share your love
     by radio, television
       and personal witness.

Such Life!

Lord,
    we praise you
        for the vigorous life
            of the Church in Brazil,
    for the urgent desire
        of Christians
        to make disciples
        and plant churches.

Lord,
    answer their prayers
        for new workers
        to help
        in the growing
        towns of Brazil.

For Santa Catarina and Rio Grande do Sul

"Serve one another in love."
GALATIANS 5:13

A great challenge, Lord,
in these two southern states
    of Brazil,
an evangelistic challenge
unlike that in other parts
    of the country,
requiring
    different methods,
    fresh ideas,
    new approaches,
testing the ingenuity
    of pastor, evangelist and teacher;
and as we ask you
to prepare church leaders
    and members
to cope with their missionary tasks,
remind them that all schemes
    are nothing
unless they help Christians
to serve their neighbours
    in love.

Protecting God's World

"Now God has his dwelling place with mankind." REVELATION 21:3

Lord,
we have focused our attention
on Brazil,
condemning
    the rape of the environment,
    the destruction of the forest,
    the pollution of the rivers,
and that's easy,
from a distance
when we don't have to find
    somewhere to live,
    somewhere to grow food,
    some way to support a family.

So, Lord,
we pray for a way of showing to people
    that this is your world,
    that you are very close to men and women
        in Jesus Christ,
        and that it is possible to live in it
           without destroying it
        when we turn to you,
        our Creator and our Father God.

Giving Thanks

*". . . in the name of our Lord Jesus
Christ give thanks every day for
everything to our God and Father."*
EPHESIANS 5:20

Lord God,
it's not hard to complain,
to find fault everywhere
    and with everyone,
to grumble at all the problems and pain
    which press hard
    on the lives of men and women,
to despair at the way human beings
    treat each other.

Then we look at Christians in Brazil,
    where life is hard,
    where many are poor,
and there is so much joy,
so much thanksgiving
    for all that you have done,
    for all that you are doing,
        through Jesus Christ
to change their lives
and to give hope for the future.

Lord, help us to join with them
every day
in giving thanks to you
for everything.

CARIBBEAN

"God is love" –
you are love –
that's easy to say
but how can people know
such words are true
    unless they see your love
      expressed in Christian lives,
    unless fine words of faith
      are backed by brave and
        caring deeds?

We thank you, Lord,
that in the Caribbean
your liberating word of love has
   meaning still
incarnate in each island church
set free in worship, care and mission
to reach the lives of all in need.

CENTRAL AMERICA

Lord,
we praise you that
   in the midst of the struggle
   for justice and peace
many Christians in Central America
have discovered the presence
   of a personal
   and loving God;
we thank you for
   their joy and gratitude
   their friendship and generosity,
   their humility and mutual care –
gifts from their Lord
who called them
to be witnesses
   among a suffering people.

MIDDLE EAST

"Salaam",
"Shalom",
words of greeting
words of peace
in the Middle East,
where there is no peace,
where people die
   from sudden attack
   and terrorist bomb,
where hostages linger
   in makeshift cells
   and wonder why
   and wonder how
   they can make the difference
   to a dispute that governments
   cannot and
   will not solve.

"Salaam",
"Shalom",
words of greeting,
words of peace
in the Holy Land,
where the Prince of Peace
once walked
and lived
and loved
and died
   for the peace,
   for the sake
     of the world.

Dear Lord,
true peace,
your peace
is no easy peace,
so give the nations
of the Middle East
the courage to set aside
   their pride,
   their anger,
   their feelings of injustice,
to meet and work and live together,
to banish war,
to bring that day
   where each can sit in safety
      under his own fig tree.

Meditations
and Prayers for
Special Occasions

Meditations and Prayers for Special Occasions

The title of this section is self-explanatory. Most of the material has been written for particular times or for special services. Some of the meditations, when used in public acts of worship, are better read by several voices.

Visitors

Father of us all,
we pray for all visitors from overseas,
    some alone and insecure,
    some amazed at our affluence,
    some made cynical by our materialism.

May they receive the best
    from our universities and colleges,
    from our churches and communities,
        and by the skills and experience they gain
        may they, in time,
            serve their own people well.

May they find friendship
    from those they meet,
    a welcome in our homes,
        and a place in our churches.

May they make a full contribution
    to the life of British churches,
    and may bonds be formed
    that will lead to understanding
    and to the growth of the Church,
        at home and overseas.

                      ★   ★   ★

Father of us all,
    we pray for visitors from overseas
        who are finding the "culture shock"
            of Britain hard to face
        and the life and worship of the churches
            so different from what they are used to
                back home.

As they study and enter into the fellowship
        of British churches
may they know that you are with them,
        teaching many new things;
help them, also, to understand
            how much they can offer to British Christians
            out of the richness of their own
                traditions and experience.

Just in Joy

Why can't we have a Christmas like we used to have,
with carols soundly sung in church and street;
a Christmas full of joy and noise,
of beaming face and laughing voice,
and choirs hitting hard the angels' chord?

Why can't we have a Christmas like we used to have,
without the stress on needy, poor and lost,
when we could eat our turkey, pud and chocs
and have no picture of a refugee
to conjure up an indigestive thought?

Why can't we have a Christmas without guilt,
no nagging doubt or hurtful conscience prick,
but just in joy to worship him
who came from God to live in love with us?

We can't – because each Christmas must be both!
The news is there for all to hear
of hunger, sorrow, homelessness and death,
and Christ was born to tell us that God cares
about the fate of human life:
his stable is the home of all earth's poor.

So, Hallelujah! Praise the Lord!
God send us forth in joy this Christmas–time
to tell the world in carol and in deed
the love of Bethlehem stable long ago,
the love which reaches through all time –
till now.

Holy Week

Father,
we come to this week with mixed feelings.
With the Jerusalem crowds we would shout and cry
"hosanna" as our King enters the city.
With them we would acknowledge our deliverer.

But we cannot be with them all the way –
We know what this leads to,
   and we are sad –
sad at his impending betrayal,
sad at the injustice of his arrest and the mockery
   of his trial,
sad at his inevitable progress to the cross,
sad for our sin and the sin of the world,
   which has placed our Lord in such a situation.

Yet we rejoice!
   for our vision sees much further.
We see your hand, O God, working great things.
We see Christ,
   not cowering before the world's might,
   but noble in victory, as, in death, he deals boldly
     with evil,
   bringing out life's everlasting light from
   death's sinful shadows.

So, Hallelujah,
Praise him who comes in the name of the Lord!

Easter

"Christ is risen" –
not empty words
echoing
from a past
and misty age,
but words of meaning
sung
by those
whose lives
know
Christ's healing touch
today,
reborn
in Easter love
and hope.
"Christ is risen!
Alleluia!"

Cry Freedom

Lord,
you cry "freedom"
all the time,
dispelling illness by your touch,
dismissing prejudice by your word,
destroying death on your cross.

Lord,
your gift is "freedom",
the resurrection freedom
of liberated life.
Help us to use your gift
to "cry freedom"
in our turn
and to bring
your peace and justice
into a world
which cries out
to be free.

I Am the Bread of Life

The Bread of Life, Lord?
Not bread, Lord, it's so ordinary!
We queue for bread in the shops,
   jostled by this one and that,
     each asking for the family choice:
       a sliced loaf; a crusty loaf;
       a wrapped loaf; a brown loaf;
       a long loaf; a short loaf;
       a milk loaf; a nutty loaf,
         and a whole-wheat loaf.

You, the Bread of Life?
Why bread, Lord?
Bread is so ordinary!
Toast at breakfast with the children,
doorstep slice and cheese with mates at work,
     picnic party,
     ladies' tea,
     hurried lunch in a London park,
     hasty snack on fast-moving train.
Bread is so ordinary, Lord.

The Bread of Life, Lord?
Why not the spice of life,
or the cake of life,
or the precious jewel of life . . . ?
But bread . . . it's so ordinary.
Everyone in every place,
     in all walks of life,
     humble and high,
     rich and poor . . .
everyone eats bread!

Are you not different, select, precious?
Are you to be shared by the rabble of humanity?
Do you belong . . . can you belong, in the
      ordinary comings and goings of life?
Can we not keep you special
      in the sacrament,
      in the sanctuary,
      in a precious religious corner,
            overvalued and useless?

The Bread of Life, Lord?
Is this what you mean?
You are for everyone,
      in every place,
      at all times,
to satisfy the hunger after real life,
      and not pander to pointless piety?

After the Storm

And the wind blew,
a terrible wind,
tearing off the roof,
whirling away the walls
of fragile shacks
that passed for homes.

And the sea surged,
violent and vicious,
sweeping through shattered villages,
carrying animals and people
in its flood
to drown in fields of sodden crops.

And after the storm
those left behind
sat stunned and shocked
amongst the debris
part of the debris,
helpless
to clear up the mess,
to see any future,
to live again.

And after the storm
they came in their hordes
from the affluent west,
with notebook and camera
and curious, prying eyes,
to feed the unending hunger
for news of human tragedy
out there,
away from home,

in a remote place
where disasters always happen.

And for ten days
they told the story,
bouncing pictures
from satellite to TV screen,
of dead and dying,
of sick and crying
of hungry,
helpless victims of the storm.

And for ten days
people gave their pennies
and their pounds
to help and feed,
to reconstruct
the lives of those
who nearly died.

And after ten days
the cameras went
as quickly as they came,
to focus on a new event
ten thousand miles away.

And after the storm
those who cannot leave
stay trapped in a cycle of poverty,
victims of climate and geography
forgotten by the wider world
until the next storm
blows away their homes and hopes
once more.

And after the storm,
as before the storm
and during the storm,
there is the Church,
God's handful of caring people,
working like leaven
in a doughy mass,
the sorry mess
of a nation's tragedy.

And after the storm
God's servants,
seeking no headline
and always with the people,
live the good news of God's love.

In the ploughing of fields
and the sowing of seed,
in the planting of trees
and the growing of food,
they live the good news
of God's love.

In the feeding of a child
and the healing of the sick,
in the caring of the old
and the comforting of sad,
they show the good news
of God's love.

In the teaching of a school
and the making of new jobs,
in the building up of lives
and the giving of fresh hope,
they share the good news
of God's love.

In the singing of glad songs
and the preaching of the Word,
in the planting of a church
and in speaking out for Christ,
they tell the good news
of God's love.

In being there with people,
in the sharing of their lives,
in standing with the reject poor
facing suffering and pain,
they are the good news
of God's love.

And after the storm,
as before the storm
and during the storm,
there is the Church,
God's handful of caring people,
always there,
seeking no headline,
wanting nothing for themselves,
but looking to you and me,
their brothers and sisters
in God's worldwide family,
for prayer and concern and support
that is constant and sure,
that does not depend
on the screams of the press,
but streams from Christ's love
in our hearts.

Speak, Lord

It's all very well
to come to church,
as we have done today,
to sing those hymns about the faith
of Wesley, Watts and all those other men,
who lived in time of pony-cart
and candlelight.

And just as well
it is,
to read that book
about the lives of men in ancient times,
who never saw a motorcar
or heard the turning record's strident sound.

I've read about those men
and know that God was very real,
and spoke in words of meaning
that could change them
into brave and brilliant souls.

But that was yesterday,
a time long lost on history's page.
I, I live now
in 1992!
and want to know if God speaks plain
   to me,
   to you,
   to everybody here,
   in twentieth-century words
we all can understand.

God Echo

God echo
sounding from the past,
        a shout,
        a speech,
        a song,
once plainly heard,
but now a wasting whisper
lost within the noise of rampant life.

Index